Bibliographical Series
of Supplements to 'British Book News'
on Writers and Their Work

★

GENERAL EDITOR
Bonamy Dobrée

THE DETECTIVE STORY IN BRITAIN

by JULIAN SYMONS

PUBLISHED FOR
THE BRITISH COUNCIL
and the NATIONAL BOOK LEAGUE
by LONGMANS, GREEN & CO.

LONGMANS, GREEN & CO. LTD.
48 Grosvenor Street, London, W.1
Railway Crescent, Croydon, Victoria, Australia
Auckland, Kingston (Jamaica), Lahore, Nairobi

LONGMANS SOUTHERN AFRICA (PTY) LTD.
Thibault House, Thibault Square, Cape Town
Johannesburg, Salisbury

LONGMANS OF NIGERIA LTD.
W. R. Industrial Estate, Ikeja

LONGMANS OF GHANA LTD.
Industrial Estate, Ring Road South, Accra

LONGMANS, GREEN (FAR EAST) LTD.
443 Lockhart Road, Hong Kong

LONGMANS OF MALAYA LTD.
44 Jalan Ampang, Kuala Lumpur

ORIENT LONGMANS LTD.
Calcutta, Bombay, Madras
Delhi, Hyderabad, Dacca

LONGMANS CANADA LTD.
137 Bond Street, Toronto 2

First published in 1962
© Julian Symons 1962

PR
830
.D4
S9

Printed in Great Britain by
F. Mildner & Sons, London, E.C.1

CONTENTS

I.	THE NATURE OF THE FORM	page 7
II.	THE BEGETTERS	10
III.	SHERLOCK HOLMES	13
IV.	THE GREAT DETECTIVE	18
V.	FAIR PLAY, AND THE REVOLT AGAINST IT	22
VI.	THE WEAKENING FORM	28
VII.	TOWARDS THE CRIME NOVEL	32
VIII.	CONCLUSION	34
	A Select Bibliography	36

ILLUSTRATIONS

I. Wilkie Collins (1824-1889) after a portrait by J. E. Millais of 1850 in the National Portrait Gallery.

II. Sir Arthur Conan Doyle (1859-1930).

III. Dorothy Sayers (1893-1957).

IV. Agatha Christie.

between pages 24 and 25

¶ Reconstruction of the living room at 221b Baker Street. Drawing by Ronald Searle. Reproduced by permission of *Punch*, page 14.

THE DETECTIVE STORY IN BRITAIN

(I) THE NATURE OF THE FORM

AS a literary form, the detective story has a place of importance in twentieth century English literature. It is important, first of all, through sheer weight of volumes. Several hundred detective stories or crime stories have been produced each year for the past forty years, and their total sales in paperback editions probably exceed those of any other sort of literature. It is well known that they are a favoured form of reading among British politicians and clerics who regard them (the compliment is ambiguous) as an agreeable relaxation from the cares of life. A small minority of them have a claim to be considered on level terms with other imaginative literature, but they receive little critical attention, and certainly most of them are not very well written. They are, however, likely to have considerable significance for future sociologists trying to interpret the nature of twentieth century man.

First of all, what is a detective story? What does an intelligent reader look for when he opens a book which is called by that name? He expects to find a situation in which a crime has been committed, and in which there is doubt about the means, the motive and the criminal. The crime may be of any kind, but in nine cases out of ten it is murder. The most important thing about the story will always be the puzzle that is set to the reader. Certain rules govern the formulation of this puzzle, and the revelation of the criminal.

The intelligent reader assumes that the writer will be fair to him. Without formulating the idea very exactly, he expects that a fair trail of clues will be laid, and that the author will not be deliberately misleading or untruthful, although the characters may lie as much as they wish. The reader will be annoyed if unsuspected facts are suddenly revealed at the end of the book. He is likely to say to a friend, if provocation has been carried far enough, that the author has 'cheated'. He may be annoyed, also, if a book which is called a detective story turns out to be a thriller.

A detective story, then, is not a thriller. A detective story asks questions about Who, Why and When; a thriller, dealing also in violent matters, simply tells us How. The lines of demarcation are sometimes vague, but books which can be classed quite positively as thrillers have been omitted from this survey. This is no denigration of John Buchan, Eric Ambler, and many other admirable writers, but simply an acknowledgement of the fact that there is a difference in kind between the two forms.

It becomes apparent to a student, however, that our intelligent reader's view of the detective story is a partial one: that the crime was not always murder, that the detective story was at first generally a short story and only latterly a novel, and that the rules he invokes when he says indignantly that the author has cheated held sway only for a period of some twenty years, between the two World Wars. During this period, which is sometimes called the Golden Age of the detective story, conventions as strict as those of Restoration comedy were established. Those writers invited to become members of the Detection Club had to swear, on their initiation, that they would abjure the use of twin brothers, secret passages and mysterious Chinamen, and exact rules were drawn up by various critics and writers, which we shall consider in detail a little later on. The detective story, as established within these conventions, was an exercise in logic. At a fairly advanced point in it the author should ideally have been able to say to the reader: 'All the clues to the puzzle are in your possession. Interpret them correctly, and they will lead to one inevitable solution.'

The pleasure the intelligent reader gets from reading detective stories is thus partly the fascination of engaging in a battle of wits with the author, something more nearly akin to a game of chess or a crossword puzzle than to the emotional rewards commonly looked for in reading fiction. But that is only the acknowledged part of the pleasure: the rest of it, often unacknowledged, rests in the fact that detective stories are concerned with violent crime. It would be facile to say simply that respectable readers sublimate their own tendencies towards violence by reading about it in detective stories. Nevertheless, the form arose in the latter part of the nineteenth century, its increasing popularity ran parallel to the development of the police force in Britain, and it does seem to be true that a high degree of personal security is necessary to the full enjoyment of the detective story.

In a social sense the detective story expresses in an extreme form the desire of the middle and upper classes in British society for a firm, almost hierarchical, social order, and for an efficient police force. Classical detective stories, with their strict rules, their invariable punishment of subtle and intelligent wrongdoers, and their bloodhound policemen supplemented when necessary by private detectives of almost superhuman intelligence and insight, are the fairy tales of Western industrial civilization. Mr. Nicholas Blake puts it extremely well when he suggests that some anthropologist of the next century may consider the detective story primarily as an outlet for the sense of guilt:

> He will call attention to the pattern of the detective-novel, as highly formalised as that of a religious ritual, with its initial necessary sin (the murder), its victim, its high priest (the criminal) who must in turn be destroyed by a yet higher power (the detective). He will conjecture—and rightly—that the devotee identified himself both with the detective and the murderer, representing the light and the dark sides of his own nature.

Mr. Blake is writing about the detective stories of the Golden Age. But this is the most curious of literary forms. Most of the greatest masters have been ignorant of or heretical about the rules; and these rules are generally disregarded to-day.

(II) THE BEGETTERS

Some historians of the detective story have found its origins in Archimedes' discovery of his principle in hydrostatics, or in the deductions by which Voltaire's Zadig was able accurately to describe the King's horse and the Queen's dog by the traces they had left behind them, but these are mere fragments of deductive reasoning. The tales of terror that were so popular in England at the end of the eighteenth century, with their emphasis on supernatural appearances and on the romantic qualities of ruined castles and sinister aristocrats, have also only the most tenuous links with the severe logic of the detective story. The father of detective fiction, in any serious sense, was undoubtedly Edgar Allan Poe. It was a freakish chance that made the generator of this conspicuously British literary form an American, but Poe was a rarity, a writer of original genius who was deeply interested in cryptograms and in the processes of deduction, and who was fascinated also by violent death. In his *Tales of Mystery and Imagination* may be found many of the elements that later writers developed. 'The Gold Bug' depends upon the solution of a cryptogram; 'Thou Art the Man' offers the most unlikely person as the criminal; and the three tales involving the Chevalier C. Auguste Dupin show him as the first 'great detective' of fiction. Dupin is a nobleman, a man of culture, and a thinking machine. We are told little of his appearance, but a great deal about his methods of reasoning. See how cunningly Poe introduces the solution to a story right at the beginning of 'The Purloined Letter', when the prefect of the Paris police comes to see Dupin and tells him of the problem of a stolen letter, a problem which is, as he says, simple yet extraordinarily baffling:

'Perhaps it is the very simplicity of the thing which puts you at fault', said my friend.

'What nonsense you *do* talk!' replied the prefect, laughing heartily.

'Perhaps the mystery is a little *too* plain', said Dupin.

'Oh, good heavens! who ever heard of such an idea?'

'A little *too* self-evident.'

'Ha! ha! ha!—ha! ha! ha!—ho! ho! ho!' roared our visitor, profoundly amused; 'oh, Dupin, you will be the death of me yet!'

The police know that the letter is hidden in a certain house. They have probed cushions with fine needles, unscrewed chair legs, opened packages and parcels, measured the thicknesses of book covers, looked beneath carpets and floor boards, examined the joints of pieces of furniture—and have overlooked what is beneath their noses. The letter, torn almost in two, has been placed with apparent carelessness in 'a trumpery filigree card-rack'. Dupin, understanding the daring of the man he is dealing with, discovers it immediately.

Poe died in 1849, and his influence upon English writers was at first indirect. Charles Dickens and Wilkie Collins, the first important writers in this country to use detective themes, owe very little to Poe. Dickens was deeply interested in the work of the recently-established detective police force, and wrote several articles about it for the magazine he edited, *Household Words*. He created the first detective in English fiction, 'Inspector Bucket of the Detective', who plays a minor but important part in *Bleak House*, and is even permitted a chapter in which he recounts the course of his deductions. Dickens, however, never wrote a detective story. His last book, *The Mystery of Edwin Drood*, offers problems which even now are not definitively solved, but it is a mystery only because it remained unfinished.

The honour of writing the first detective novel (for Poe wrote only short stories in the field of detection) belongs to Dickens's close friend and occasional collaborator, Wilkie Collins. The book is *The Moonstone*, and the year of its appearance 1868. Mr. T. S. Eliot has called *The Moonstone* the first and best detective story, and certainly it is an original and fascinating book, notable because of its wonderfully ingenious construction, and also because Collins anticipated the standards of fair play already mentioned, which at the time he wrote were of course unknown. As Dorothy Sayers has pointed out, almost every clue needed for solution of the mystery is set out in the early chapters, and although the solution itself may be disappointing to our sophisticated tastes, it is perfectly fair. Collins's professional detective, Sergeant Cuff, is based upon Sergeant Whicher of the detective department. He is described with loving care by the house-steward, Gabriel Betteredge:

> A fly from the railway drove up as I reached the lodge; and out got a grizzled, elderly man so lean that he looked as if he had not got an ounce of flesh on his bones in any part of him. He was dressed all in decent black, with a white cravat round his neck. His face was as sharp as a hatchet, and the skin of it was as yellow and dry and withered as an autumn leaf. His eyes, of a steely light grey, had a very disconcerting trick, when they encountered your eyes, of looking as if they expected something more from you than you were aware of yourself. His walk was soft; his voice was melancholy; his long lanky fingers were hooked like claws. He might have been a parson, or an undertaker—or anything else you like, except what he really was.

Cuff is the first master of the apparently irrelevant report, the unexpected observation. Faced with a difficult problem and asked what is to be done, he trims his nails with a penknife and suggests a turn in the garden and a look at the roses; asked who has stolen the missing yellow diamond that gives a title to the book he says blandly that nobody has stolen it. The fascination of such remarks is that their meaning just eludes us. By making the proper deductions we feel that we should be able to grasp it.

Collins, who wrote a number of other novels and short stories with some detective interest, as well as the masterly thriller *The Woman in White*, did not realise that he was working in a new form. He would have been astonished by the distinction made to-day between the 'serious' novel and the detective story which is regarded as being, to quote one of the few historians of the *genre*, Mr. Howard Haycraft, 'a frankly non-serious, entertainment form of literature'. Collins might have been moved to indignation by such a remark, and so might the other masters in this period who dealt with detective themes, Poe, Dickens, the Frenchman Emile Gaboriau (whose detective, Lecoq, is modelled partly on Dupin and partly on Vidocq, the ex-convict who founded the Sûretè), and the under-rated Irish novelist Sheridan Le Fanu, who wrote two remarkable detective stories *Wylder's Hand* and *The House By The Churchyard*. The radical change, through which the detective story was regarded as a 'frankly non-serious' form of literature came with Sherlock Holmes.

(III) SHERLOCK HOLMES

The first Sherlock Holmes story was the novel, *A Study in Scarlet*, written by Dr. Arthur Conan Doyle in 1886 and published in the following year. A second novel, *The Sign of Four*, appeared three years later. The first series of short stories appeared in the *Strand Magazine* in 1891, and they brought instant and immense success to their author. At the end of the second series, Holmes and Moriarty went to their presumed deaths over the Reichenbach Falls, and Doyle wrote thankfully to a friend that he had killed off his hero:

> I have had such an overdose of him that I feel towards him as I do towards *pâté de foie gras*, of which I once ate too much, so that the name of it gives me a sickly feeling to this day.

14 THE DETECTIVE STORY IN BRITAIN

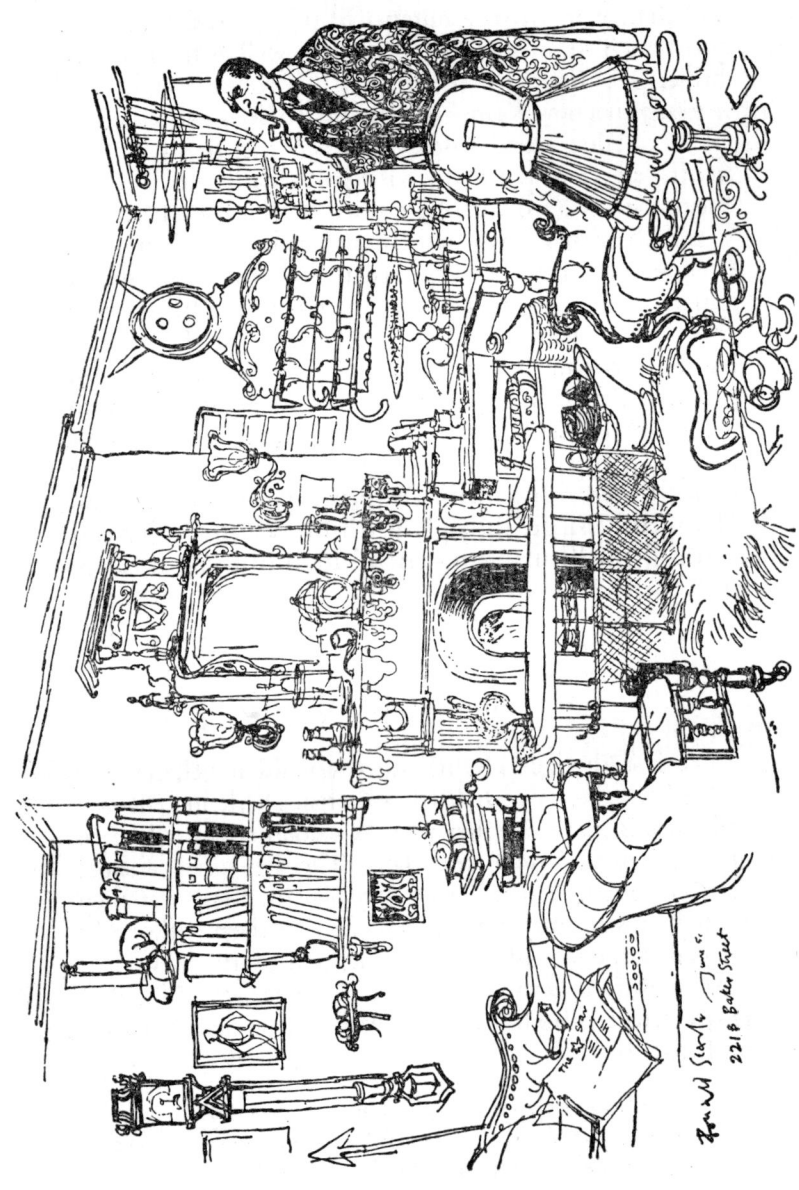

But the insistence of readers, and Doyle's own need for money, brought Holmes back in three more collections of short stories and two more novels. Doyle wrote several admirable historical novels, and it was by these that he wished and expected to be remembered. The fact that his fame, as the years passed, rested more and more upon the Holmes stories, was something to which he never became reconciled. 'I have never taken them seriously myself', he wrote, and he made a sharp distinction between his serious fiction and what he regarded as the trivia of the Holmes stories. In vain: as a writer Conan Doyle was the victim of the legend he had so casually created.

Within a very short time Sherlock Holmes became a legend so vivid that criminal or emotional problems were addressed to him for solution, and pilgrimages made in search of his consulting rooms at 221b Baker Street. Doyle wrote many of the early short stories quickly, without worrying about consistencies of date in the history of his hero or of his faithful chronicler, Doctor Watson. From these inconsistencies there grew and flourished, after Doyle's death in 1930, a whole literature dealing with such matters as Holmes's interest in music, his relations with women, his early life and career as a student. There is a smaller, but still considerable, literature devoted to Watson. There is even a London public house called the 'Sherlock Holmes' where the sitting room at Baker Street, complete with its occupant, may be regarded while one dines, and where many mementoes of Holmes's famous cases are preserved on the walls of the saloon bar. With Holmes the Great Detective really came to flower.

The Great Detective has certain strongly marked characteristics, which fascinated Victorian and Edwardian readers because they were so alien to their own deep-seated respectability. He is eccentric and often anti-social; Holmes, when we are first introduced to him takes drugs, and has fits of depression when he lies upon a sofa 'for days on end . . . hardly uttering a word or moving a muscle from morning to night'. He plays the violin extremely well, but when left to himself will merely 'scrape carelessly at the fiddle thrown across his knee'. He is also deeply and narrowly egotistical. When Watson expresses astonishment that Holmes is ignorant of the Copernican theory and of the composition of the Solar System, Holmes says that such information can be of no use to him:

> 'But the Solar System!' I protested.
> 'What the deuce is it to me?' he interrupted impatiently. 'You say that we go round the sun. If we went round the moon it would not make a pennyworth of difference to me or to my work.'

The Great Detective is above, or at any rate outside, human emotions:

> He was, I take it, the most perfect reasoning and observing machine that the world has seen: but as a lover, he would have placed himself in a false position. He never spoke of the softer passions, save with a gibe and a sneer ... Grit in a sensitive instrument, or a crack in one of his own high-power lenses, would not be more disturbing than a strong emotion in a nature such as his.

In later stories Doyle found it necessary to soften and humanise Holmes's nature, but there can be no doubt that his presentation as an eccentric genius was part of his attraction; and attractive, too, in a highly conventional society, was Holmes's readiness to place himself above the the law. In 'The Abbey Grange' Holmes and Watson jointly decide that they will not reveal to the police the identity of the man who killed Sir Eustace Brackenstall; in 'Charles Augustus Milverton' they actually see a woman shoot the man who is blackmailing her, grind her heel into his upturned face, and do nothing about it; in 'The Blue Carbuncle' Holmes condones a felony with the reflection that it is possible he is saving a soul. In these, and in some other cases, Holmes has decided that the law is not adequate to mete out justice, and that he must do so himself. This dangerous doctrine is endorsed by other Great Detectives, including Chesterton's Father Brown, Dorothy Sayers's Lord Peter Wimsey and the American S. S. van Dine's Philo Vance. The exploits of Sherlock Holmes fulfilled much the same psychological function for their early readers that those of Superman fulfil to-day.

To stress the psychological basis of the Holmes legend is not to deny that these are excellent stories. Something in Doyle's Victorian romanticism responded to the figure he was inventing, and in the creation of Sherlock Holmes he wrought better than he knew. The character based originally on Doyle's old teacher Joseph Bell, the consulting surgeon at Edinburgh's Royal Infirmary, was enlarged far beyond the scope of Bell's character or deductive abilities. Doyle perfected the puzzling but meaningful retort, and used it with a skill that no other writer of detective stories has ever approached.

> 'Is there any other point to which you would wish to draw my attention?'
> 'To the curious incident of the dog in the night-time.'
> 'The dog did nothing in the night-time.'
> 'That was the curious incident', remarked Sherlock Holmes.

The dog did not bark, although somebody had entered the stables where he was on watch, and had taken out a horse. The significance of the incident is that the intruder must have been somebody well known to the dog.

Holmes is also unequalled in the brilliant deductions he is able to make from apparently trifling pieces of evidence. Given a battered old black felt hat, of which Watson can make nothing, he says:

> 'That the man was highly intellectual is of course obvious upon the face of it, and also that he was fairly well-to-do within the last three years, although he has now fallen upon evil days. He had foresight, but has less now than formerly, pointing to a moral retrogression, which, when taken with the decline of his fortunes, seems to indicate some evil influence, probably drink, at work upon him. This may account also for the obvious fact that his wife has ceased to love him.'

It is not surprising that Watson exclaims, 'My dear Holmes!' But Holmes has a reasonable basis for these, and for the six other deductions that he makes from the battered hat. Very often it would be easy to reach different conclusions, but in our dazed pleasant astonishment at Holmes's skill we do not notice that until afterwards.

The formula to which many of Holmes's exploits were written—the introduction of a new client, either by letter or in person, Holmes's startling deductions from very fragmentary evidence, the introduction of the other characters and the setting of the puzzle, Holmes's enigmatic remarks in relation to it, and the final solution—is perfectly suited to the short story form, much less well to the novel. Of the four Holmes novels, only *The Hound of the Baskervilles* is a real success, and this less for the puzzle, which is not difficult to solve, than for the skill with which Doyle makes us feel the terror and loneliness of the Devon moors, implied in the disturbed feelings of the sane and sober doctor who discovered footprints beside the dead body of Sir Charles Baskerville. A man's or a woman's footprints? Holmes asks, and Doctor Mortimer almost whispers his reply:

'Mr. Holmes, they were the footprints of a gigantic hound!'

The romantic excitement we feel in the Holmes stories springs from the strength with which Doyle conceived this vanished world of hansom cabs and gas lamps, of fogs and impenetrable disguises, of an incognito King of Bohemia and of the great coal-black hound whose "muzzle and hackles and dewlap were outlined in flickering flame."

(IV) THE GREAT DETECTIVE

The technique of the detective short story changed rapidly, and among the dozens of writers who tried to emulate the form and manner of the Holmes stories, very few are read to-day. Their stories are out-of-date, yet they lack almost entirely the period feeling that we value in the Holmes stories. Nobody to-day reads the work of Arthur Morrison, whose Martin Hewitt stories were at one time popular; or of McDonnell Bodkin, who created the first lady detective, Dora Myrl, and also the first father and son detective collaboration, in young Beck and his father; nor is it easy to find Baroness Orczy's ingenious tales about *The Old Man in the Corner*, who claims that 'there is no such thing as a mystery in connection with any crime, provided intelligence is brought to bear upon its investigation', and who solves a number of crimes without moving from his place in the corner of an A.B.C. teashop; nor the short stories which recount the exploits of Ernest Bramah's blind detective Max Carrados, who like Holmes is given to amending the law, in one case to the point of ordering a murderer to commit suicide. Few nowadays look at the books of the once-famous R. Austin Freeman, a doctor who created the first truly scientific detective in Doctor Thorndyke. It is a pity that Thorndyke is so nearly lost to us, because Freeman was an innovator of importance who wrote, in *The Singing Bone*, a collection of 'inverted' stories, in which we see a crime committed and then watch Thorndyke reveal the criminal, with the aid of the square green box covered with Willesden canvas, in which he keeps an extraordinary variety of materials for the detection of crime. The truth is, however, that Freeman, like many of his fellows, was an extremely poor writer, and in the end it is the quality of the writing that preserves all forms of art. In G. K. Chesterton's Father Brown stories the plots are often of dazzling ingenuity, but it is above all the zest and sparkle of the writing that makes us return to them again and again with pleasure.

In one of his essays Chesterton says that 'of (the) realisation of a great city itself as something wild and obvious the detective story is certainly the *Iliad*. The lights of the city are the guardians of some secret, however crude, which the writer knows and the reader does not. Every twist of the road is like a finger pointing to it; every fantastic skyline of chimney-pots seems wildly and derisively signalling the meaning of the mystery.'

This is wonderful special pleading for Chesterton's own stories. His dumpy little Catholic priest-detective, who finds difficulty in rolling his umbrella and does not know the right end of his return ticket, is the most preposterous of detectives. He is made acceptable by the genius that places him among scenes which also outrage realism: a secret garden where there are found two severed heads but only one body; a desolate house in the West Country in which the body of a man looking like an enormous bat is found spreadeagled among unspotted snow. In Chesterton's stories we meet stars that fly, feet that bound along a corridor like those of a panther and then change to a slow shuffling tread, an image in a passage which appears differently to each witness. In the field of detection Chesterton wrote only short stories, and the first two of his five collections, *The Innocence of Father Brown* and *The Wisdom of Father Brown* are much the best. Chesterton was a Catholic convert, and it has been said that he carried his faith too much and too obviously into his detective stories, but really the complaint seems a churlish one. If we accept Father Brown as a character—and Chesterton makes us do so—then we must accept also the fact that he is a priest, who may draw from any crime its religious moral. Chesterton is not a model for any other writer to copy, and the later logicians of the detective story, who drew up the 'fair play' rules, complained bitterly that Chesterton outraged them all, that he would not tell you whether all the windows were fastened or whether a shot in the gun-room could be heard in the butler's pantry. But the genius of Chesterton lay in his ability to ignore all that, to leave out everything extraneous to the single theme he wanted to develop, and yet to provide us with a clue that is blindingly obvious once we have accepted the premises of the story.

A dog whines because a stick sinks in the sea, the red light from a closed door looks like 'a splash of blood that grew vivid as it cried for vengeance', the priest of a new religion does not look round when he hears a crash and a scream, and these are clues by which we may solve mysteries if we have wit enough to understand them.

The detective story is particularly rich, if that is the word, in books which are of historical importance, although they are no longer of much interest to modern readers. Pre-eminent among them is *Trent's Last Case*, written by Chesterton's friend E. C. Bentley, and published in 1913. It is difficult nowadays to account for the high regard in which this book was held for many years. The writing seems stiff and characterless, the movement from one surprise to another, and the final shock of revelation, rather artificial. Perhaps it was the fact that Philip Trent, the detective, was such an ordinary human being that gave the book its great popularity. Mr. Howard Haycraft has remarked perceptively that 'its deceptive *un*-remarkableness, in fact, is the chief reason for its uniqueness in an era in which flamboyance and over-writing were the hall-marks of the crime novel'.

To-day A. E. W. Mason's first detective story, *At The Villa Rose*, published three years before Bentley's book, seems much more interesting than *Trent's Last Case*. Mason was an accomplished novelist, who wrote also four books, in which, as he says, he tried to 'combine the crime story which produces a shiver with the detective story which aims at a surprise'. His detective is M. Hanaud of the Sûreté, a stout broad-shouldered bourgeois who looks like a prosperous comedian. His very distinctive Watson is an over-fastidious dilettante and uxorious bachelor named Ricardo, who has made a fortune in Mincing Lane and feels it a point of honour to keep himself thoroughly up to date both in his very sound knowledge of red wine and in the criminal affairs of his friend Hanaud. Of Mason's four crime stories, which were published at wide intervals, *The*

House of the Arrow is perhaps the best, but all stand the most important test applicable to the detective story: they can be read again with pleasure.

(V) FAIR PLAY AND THE REVOLT AGAINST IT

The idea that the detective story is a distinctive literary form for which rules can be laid down was formulated during the nineteen twenties by many writers, perhaps most lucidly by Father (later Monsignor) Ronald Knox. The detective story, he said, was a game between two players, 'the author of the one part and the reader of the other part', and when one talked about rules it was not 'in the sense in which poetry has rules, but . . . in the sense in which cricket has rules—a far more impressive consideration to the ordinary Englishman'. He then laid down a 'Detective Decalogue', too long to be printed in full, which is summarised here:

(i) The criminal must be mentioned early on.
(ii) Supernatural solutions are ruled out.
(iii) Only one secret room or passage is allowed.
(iv) No undiscovered poisons are permitted.
(v) No Chinamen should appear in the story.
(vi) The detective must not be helped by lucky accidents, or by intuitions.
(vii) The detective must not himself commit the crime.
(viii) Nor must he conceal clues from the reader.
(ix) The thoughts of the 'Watson' must not be concealed.
(x) There must be special warning of the use of twin brothers, or doubles.

It was easy to show by reference to the rules that the Sherlock Holmes stories erred in many ways, particularly in the matter of concealing clues from the reader. The American S. S. van Dine, the creator of Philo Vance, thought that all characterisation should be excluded from the detective story, and that 'style' had no more business in it than in a crossword puzzle.

It seems strange to-day that such rules can ever have been taken seriously, but during the years between the wars a great many writers worked carefully within them, and produced books which had almost invariably been plotted with a slide rule, but were written without style or savour. Among them were Freeman Wills Crofts, a railway construction engineer who turned to writing detective stories and specialised in apparently unbreakable alibis which were often connected with the intricacies of railway time tables; the Socialist economists G. D. H. and Margaret Cole, who like Crofts employed principally a police detective; E. R. Punshon, J. J. Connington, Ronald Knox himself, and a host of other writers now almost forgotten. To these writers, who were almost all novelists rather than short story writers, a plot constructed in accordance with the rules (and very often accompanied by a plan of the Manor House or of the library) was all; wit, characterisation, and consideration of the psychology of the people involved in the books, nothing.

The most interesting books produced by a firm adherent to the rules are undoubtedly those of John Dickson Carr, who wrote also as Carter Dickson, an American who qualifies for consideration here because his subjects and characters are so often English. Mr. Carr is a disciple of Chesterton, and his detectives, Doctor Fell and H. M., are in manner distinctly Chestertonian. He is a specialist in 'locked room' mysteries, in which an apparently impossible situation is always ingeniously resolved, and he has exceeded even his master in dramatic inventiveness. In recent years his work has shown a falling-off in quality, perhaps because of the human difficulty in ringing the changes so often on a single theme, but *The Hollow Man*, *The Black Spectacles*, and a Carter Dickson book, *The Reader is Warned*, are three books (and a dozen others almost equally as good might be mentioned) which delight us simply by their staggering ingenuity. *The Hollow Man* contains a chapter which is in effect a brilliant essay on the many varieties of locked room mysteries.

Carr is an exception. Upon the whole the flowering of talent that caused the years between the wars to be called the Golden Age came, in Britain, not by adherence to the rules but through a measure of revolt against them. The revolt came principally through three writers: Anthony Berkeley, Agatha Christie and Dorothy Sayers.

Anthony Berkeley began writing straightforward detective stories with an amateur detective named Roger Sheringham playing the central part. He soon, however, demonstrated considerable irreverence in relation to the rules. *The Poisoned Chocolates Case* offers six separate solutions to the stated problem: who sent the box of poisoned chocolates that killed Joan Bendix? In a sense this is an academically perfect puzzle, but it is also something near to a parody of the whole form. The book was published in 1929 and a year later, in the preface to *The Second Shot*, Berkeley wrote:

> I am personally convinced that the days of the old crime-puzzle, pure and simple, relying entirely upon the plot and without any added attractions of character, style, or even humour, are in the hands of the auditor; and that the detective story is in the process of developing into the novel with a detective or crime interest, holding its readers less by mathematical than by psychological ties.

In 1931, under the pseudonym of Francis Iles, he published *Malice Aforethought*, and in the following year an equally brilliant successor to it, *Before the Fact*. What was new about these books may be expressed in the first sentences of *Malice Aforethought*:

> It was not until several weeks after he had decided to murder his wife that Dr. Bickleigh took any active steps in the matter. Murder is a serious business.

I. Wilkie Collins (1824-1889) after a portrait by J. E. Millais of 1850 in the National Portrait Gallery

II. Sir Arthur Conan Doyle (1859-1930)

III. Dorothy Sayers (1893-1957) *Howard Coster*

IV. Agatha Christie

We have here not a detective story, but a crime novel. We see Doctor Bickleigh's plans for murdering his wife, the progress of those plans, the police investigation after her death. But the effect created is quite different from that of a Thorndyke 'inverted' story. The fascination of this book, and of its successor, is in the interplay of character, the gaps between plan and execution, and in the dramatic ironies permitted himself by the author. The third Iles book, *As For The Woman*, was interesting, but much inferior to the first two: and unhappily, since then both Francis Iles and Anthony Berkeley have been silent. It was a long time before Iles's approach to the crime story was to bear any considerable fruit.

Berkeley-Iles was a conscious heretic, Agatha Christie perhaps an unconscious one. In *The Murder of Roger Ackroyd*, published in 1926, she replaced her usual extraordinarily stupid Watson, Captain Hastings, with an amiable country doctor named Sheppard. The doctor's first meeting with the little Belgian private detective, Hercule Poirot, comes when a vegetable marrow is thrown over the garden wall:

> I looked up angrily. Over the wall, to my left, there appeared a face. An egg-shaped head, partially covered with suspiciously black hair, two immense moustaches, and a pair of watchful eyes.
> He broke at once into fluent apologies.
> 'I demand of you a thousand pardons, monsieur. I am without defence. For some months now I cultivate the marrows. This morning suddenly I enrage myself with these marrows. I seize the biggest. I hurl him over the wall. Monsieur, I am ashamed. I prostrate myself.'

So the relationship is established. The friendly country doctor, who is telling the story, becomes Poirot's helper. Then in the last chapter, he is revealed as the murderer. The outcry was long and loud. This, it was said, was a deliberate cheat on the reader. And one or two of Mrs. Christie's later books, like *The A.B.C. Murders* and *Ten Little Niggers*, provoked almost as much discussion. Mrs.

Christie was accused of an unscrupulous use of the least-likely-person motive, and of failure to pay attention to the probabilities and to 'the canons of fair play'. Some pundits, including S. S. van Dine, brought in a verdict of guilty, others, like Ronald Knox, were graciously 'inclined to let her off', others still, like Dorothy Sayers, cast votes for acquittal. Undisturbed by this flurry of argument, Mrs. Christie went on to produce during the nineteen thirties a whole series of books which with great ingenuity play variations on the theme of tricking the reader. The first string to her detectival bow has always been Hercule Poirot, who has become less eccentric in speech and appearance with the passing years. The second string is a quiet spinster named Miss Marple.

Mrs. Christie has become more and more tired of Poirot, but has been obliged by public demand to go on writing books about him. Miss Dorothy Sayers, by contrast, could never have enough of Lord Peter Wimsey, and one might change Wilde's epigram a little by saying that to fall in love with one's detective is the beginning of a lifelong romance. We meet Lord Peter in her first novel, *Whose Body?*, published in 1923. He is an elegant aristocrat, and a devoted bibliophile who has such faith in his man Bunter that, when criminal affairs press, he is able to send Bunter off to a sale with the vaguest instructions:

> 'I don't want to miss the Folio Dante nor the De Voragine—here you are—see? *Golden Legend*—Wynkyn de Worde, 1493—got that?—and, I say, make a special effort for the Caxton Folio of the *Four Sons of Aymon*—it's the 1489 folio and unique.'

Lord Peter then changes hurriedly to go to see an architect who has found a dead body in his bath.

> He selected a dark-green tie to match his socks and tied it accurately without hesitation or the slightest compression of his lips; substituted a pair of brown shoes for his black ones, slipped a monocle into a breast pocket, and took up a beautiful Malacca walking-stick with a heavy silver knob.

Lord Peter drops the last letters of a good many words, and uses slang which is at times reminiscent of P. G. Wodehouse's Bertie Wooster ('I'll toddle round to Battersea now an' try to console the poor little beast', he says before going round to see the architect). Miss Sayers eventually equipped him with a 'Who's Who' entry and a lengthy 'biographical note' written by his uncle, Paul Austin Delagardie, which were printed in the new editions of every book about him.

Dorothy Sayers's originality certainly did not rest in the creation of Lord Peter, who is one of the purest fragments of feminine wish-fulfilment in fiction. In her early books, indeed, she was a fairly conscientious adherent to the rules. There was, she thought, great difficulty about letting real human beings into a detective story. 'At some point or other, either their emotions make hay of the detective interest, or the detective interest gets hold of them and makes their emotions look like pasteboard.' She was particularly severe upon 'the heroes who insist on fooling about after young women when they ought to be putting their minds to the job of detection' and concluded that, upon the whole, 'the less love in a detective story, the better'.

It is doubtful if one should give more weight to Dorothy Sayers's wish to provide Lord Peter with a love affair, or to her recognition that the 'rules' were absurdly restrictive: but in her later books she strove to create real human beings, and placed no restriction upon their emotions. In *Strong Poison* Lord Peter clears Harriet Vane of a charge of murder, and falls in love with her in the process; in *Gaudy Night* a puzzle (not a murder) is blended with an account of Lord Peter's love affair, and *Busman's Honeymoon* is frankly subtitled: 'A love story with detective interruptions.' Nor was this the limit of her experimentation. Implicit in the fair play rules was the idea that the setting of a story should not be too obtrusive, since its function was simply to serve as background for the puzzle and not to provide a distracting interest in itself. The lively picture of an advertising agency in *Murder Must Advertise* disregarded this idea, and so did the picture of the Fens and the campanological lore in *The Nine Tailors*.

It cannot be said that Miss Sayers's rebellion against the rules was completely successful. Her formidable intellect and learning were perfectly employed in writing the several essays in the form that appeared as introductions to collections of 'Great Short Stories of Detection, Mystery and Horror', but she never produced the masterpiece which her admirers had expected. The plots of her best books are shaped with wonderful skill, but there seems to be a softness at the centre of them. Her infatuation with Lord Peter, and her attempt to turn the detective story into a 'novel of manners' ended in a weakening of the detective element almost to the point where it ceased to exist. In the end she became dissatisfied with what she contemptuously called "the artificial plot-construction" of her own and other people's books. During the last twenty years of her life she wrote no more detective stories, and often referred slightingly to her own work within the detective form.

(VI) THE WEAKENING FORM

> In detective fiction, as in any other *genre* of literature there comes a moment when fresh blood is needed, not only for its novelty but for its tonic effect as a whole. For some time now little has appeared, except from the pens of the old masters, which has been above a mediocre level.

So wrote the *Times Literary Supplement* reviewer in 1936, welcoming Michael Innes's first book, *Death at the President's Lodging*, which he called 'the most important contribution to detective literature that has appeared for some time'. This book and its immediate successors, *Hamlet, Revenge!* and *Stop Press* were certainly something new in detective fiction. These books followed the letter of the fair play rules in presenting a puzzle and the clues by which it might be solved, but flouted the spirit of them outrageously by a frivolity which turned the detective story into a literary conversation piece. There is no greater quotation-spotter or quotation-capper in detective literature than Inspector, later Sir John, Appleby, no conversations so recondite or so witty as those carried on by the guests at Scamnum Court, the seat of the Duke of Horton, where the Lord Chancellor is murdered during an amateur performance of *Hamlet*. Few Innes characters will flinch at playing a parlour game which involves remembering quotations about bells in Shakespeare, and Appleby, when confronted by the 'fourteen bulky volumes of the Argentorati Athenaeus' murmurs:

> 'The *Deipnosophists* . . . Schweighauser's edition . . . takes up a lot of room . . . Dindorf's compacter . . . and there he is.'

Appleby shows off sometimes in these early books, but not as Lord Peter shows off, by appearing a superior being to those surrounding him: it is rather that Appleby has to be a man of letters in order to survive in the highly cultured environment of Mr. Innes's imagination. At the time of writing these books Mr. Innes (the pseudonym of J. I. M. Stewart) was professor of English at Adelaide University. Asked to comment on his work in the field of detection he said that it had a somewhat literary flavour, and that some of his books were on the frontier between the detective story and the fantasy. Mr. Innes is now a don at Christ Church. His later detective stories are always amusing and original, but perhaps his most successful books in recent years have been thrillers, among which *The Journeying Boy* and *The Man From the Sea* should be mentioned as quite exceptionally good. His most recent detective stories lack the literary high spirits of the earlier books, and sometimes show a certain carelessness in craftsmanship. The detective story was momentarily freshened, but finally weakened, by this attempt to treat it as an occasion for a display of literary fireworks in the manner of Aldous Huxley.

Nicholas Blake belonged like Innes to the post-Sayers generation. Blake (the pseudonym of the poet Cecil Day Lewis) invented a 'literary' detective, Nigel Strangeways, who solved one mystery by his recognition of a quotation from the Jacobean dramatist, Tourneur. His first book, *A Question of Proof*, was a lively and accomplished mystery set at a boys' prep school, and his fourth, *The Beast Must Die*, which appeared in 1938, was an extraordinarily clever variation of Agatha Christie's trick in *The Murder of Roger Ackroyd*. Like Innes again, Blake at first wrote detective stories in which the most engaging thing was the bubbling high spirits of the author, the obvious pleasure he felt in playing the detective game. With the years the high spirits have faded, and too often Blake's later detective stories bear the mark of being chores rather than pleasures. But there are several of his books to which such a stricture does not apply, among them his wartime *Minute for Murder*, a post-war book set in a publishing firm and called *End of Chapter*, and *A Tangled Web*, a fictional modern reconstruction of an Edwardian murder case, which alone among Blake's books is written with intense personal feeling.

In the thirties Innes and Blake were acclaimed by their admirers as giving a new direction to the detective story, and criticised by some detractors as too highbrow. To-day both praise and detraction seem exaggerated. In their writing there is no real break with the detective story's traditional features. Both employed a detective who appeared in a series of books, and who showed much of the omniscience carried down from the days of Sherlock Holmes. Both regarded the detective story as 'entertainment' literature, in which it was not advisable to dig deeply into character or motive. Both, Innes more than Blake, ignored the events of their day and set their stories in a setting that in a political and social sense was timeless. The innovations that they made were minor, the rejection of the railway time table and eventually of the drawing showing the scene of the crime, and the abandonment of that most limited of all detective story conventions by which the body is found in the library at a house party where every guest has a reason for wishing the victim dead.

Much the same could be said of two other talented writers who came to literary maturity in the years before the war, Margery Allingham and Ngaio Marsh. Both used a detective, in Miss Allingham's case the aristocratic amateur Albert Campion, in Miss Marsh's the gentlemanly, unobtrusive professional Detective-Inspector (later Superintendent) Roderick Alleyn; both wrote with an ease and elegance unknown to the stricter purists of the fair play school; both were prepared to investigate the psychology of their characters, and also to provide a background which was seen with a most agreeably satirical eye. Miss Allingham's progress has been particularly interesting. She began with some light-hearted and rather sentimental books in which Campion seems at times almost a figure of caricature:

> The Inspector had a vision of a lank immaculate form surmounted by a pale face half obliterated by enormous horn-rimmed spectacles. The final note of incongruity was struck by an old-fashioned deerstalker cap set jauntily upon the top of the young man's head.

That is Campion in 1931, in *Police at the Funeral*. Here he is fourteen years later, in *Coroner's Pidgin*, after some arduous war service:

> He had changed a little in the past three years; the sun had bleached his fair hair to whiteness lending him a physical distinction he had never before possessed. There were new lines in his over-thin face and with their appearance some of his old misleading vacancy of expression had vanished. But nothing had altered the upward drift of his thin mouth nor the engaging astonishment which so often and so falsely appeared in his pale eyes.

Campion has not merely aged and matured; he is regarded with deeper seriousness by his creator, and so is the world in which he moves. As the years went by Miss Allingham felt herself less and less confined by the bonds of the fair play detective story, and began to write books which in effect were novels with a detective element in them. Miss Marsh never went so far, but there was noticeable in her books also a greater interest in the settings than in the puzzles to be solved. The first third of *Overture to Death* gives a fascinating picture of the squabbles in a village about what play shall be done to raise money for the Young People's Friendly Circle, how it shall be cast and, most significant of all, who shall perform the overture. The first half of *Opening Night* gives in a rather similar way a picture of the intrigues taking place before the opening of a new play. In both of these books we are fascinated by the relationships between the characters, and want to see them developed fully. The murder, with its following investigation and interrogation of suspects, puts a halt to this process and causes a distinct lowering of our emotional temperature.

The experiments of these four writers, and some others of less importance, had little obvious effect on the apparent supremacy of the detective novel produced according to the fair play rules. It was not until a new generation of crime writers appeared, after the second World War, that the decline of the detective story as a literary form became obvious.

(VII) TOWARDS THE CRIME NOVEL

At the heart of the classical detective story, as Ronald Knox said, was the Great Detective, who appeared in story after story and created a bond of familiarity between writer and reader:

It is personality that counts (Ronald Knox wrote). You are not bound to make your public *like* the Great Detective; many readers have found Lord Peter Wimsey too much of a good thing, and I have even heard of people who were unable to appreciate the flavours of Poirot. But he must be real; he must have idiosyncrasies, eccentricities; even if he is a professional policeman, like Hanaud, he must smoke those appalling cigarettes, and get his English idioms wrong.

There could be no clearer indication of the move away from the detective story since the war than the fact that only one of the crime writers who have come into prominence during the past fifteen years has made any attempt to create a Great Detective. This is Mr. Edmund Crispin, a talented writer who would probably acknowledge Michael Innes as his exemplar. Crispin's highly individual sense of light comedy and his flair for verbal deception make all of his books extremely enjoyable. The best of them, *The Moving Toyshop*, is a most successfully mystifying frolic. But Crispin and his Professor Fen were swimming against the stream, and he has been silent now for several years. Many of the practitioners firmly established before the war have changed their approach to the detective story. Agatha Christie has trimmed Poirot's eccentricities and has abandoned altogether his faithful Watson, Captain Hastings, because she thought that Hastings seemed too ridiculous. Margery Allingham has retained Albert Campion, but his activities seem an unnecessary intrusion in *The Tiger in the Smoke* and *Hide My Eyes*, two of her most recent books. Nigel Strangeways, Sir John Appleby and Superintendent Roderick Alleyn are still active, but they are much muted nowadays, for it is the object of their creators to soften rather than to emphasise those idiosyncrasies that Ronald Knox thought so important. And it is not seriously disputed that the work of these practitioners nowadays is much below their best writing. Mr. Howard Haycraft, when asked to name books published within the last ten years which might come within the canon of the best hundred detective stories, mentioned only *The Daughter of Time*, a brilliantly freakish performance by Josephine Tey (a pseudonym of the dramatist Gordon Daviot) in which a police inspector 'solves' from his hospital bed the mystery of Richard III and the Princes in the Tower. The Detection Club, once so austerely concerned about candidates' credentials under the fair play rules, now requires from them only a high degree of professional skill.

There were two main reasons for the changed attitude of new crime writers. The first was a general feeling, earlier voiced by Dorothy Sayers, that it had become extremely difficult to devise new methods of murder and new ways of deceiving the reader. The tricks of Sherlock Holmes, protected as they are by the patina of age, still have power to fascinate us: but how ludicrous we should find it if any modern detective adopted the device used by Holmes in his attempt in *A Scandal in Bohemia* to discover Irene Adler's secret, of pretending injury in a street fight so that he may obtain entry into her house, and then having a plumber's smoke rocket thrown into the sitting room, so that she will rush to the safe that holds her secret. Proof that puzzles and deceptions have become harder to devise is not lacking in the work of such exponents of apparent impossibilities as John Dickson Carr, and in the most recent work of Agatha Christie.

(VIII) CONCLUSION

An even more potent cause of change was the fact that the post-war crime writers looked at the world in a different way from their predecessors. Behind the detective stories written before the war there was a belief that human affairs could be ruled by reason and that virtue, generally identified with the established order of society, must prevail in the end. The post war crime writers did not identify themselves with such a point of view. They saw, instead, a world in which German force had been defeated only by the greater force employed by the Allies, and in which concentration camps and the atomic bomb mocked a liberal dream of reason. The new writers had no wish to create locked room puzzles. They have turned instead to stories which, while often retaining a puzzle element, are primarily concerned with crime in relation to character and motive. We have seen what Dorothy Sayers thought about the difficulty of letting 'real human beings' enter a detective story. The compromise she effected was very much on the side of the detective story—that is to say, her human beings were not very real: but recent writers have had no hesitation in admitting 'real human beings' into their books, and working out stories of which the central interest was the investigation of human motives. They have been prepared to discuss sex with reasonable freedom (the writers of the Golden Age showed an astonishing prudishness about this most potent motive for crime), and have even been prepared to question the way in which the police treat those under suspicion. It was a tradition of the British detective story that the police might be stupid, but could never be seriously corrupt or brutal. The abandonment of this shibboleth, in such books as John Bingham's *My Name is Michael Sibley* or in my own *The Progress of a Crime* showed that the defences were really down.

The new crime novel has retained many elements of the detective story, but its interests are much more like those of a novel. It looks back to Francis Iles, much more than to Conan Doyle or Dorothy Sayers. Its practitioners vary in style, feeling and treatment. They include Margot Bennett, who writes at her best with a wit and elegance lacking in a great many 'serious' novelists, Edward Grierson whose best work stems fairly directly from Francis Iles, Shelley Smith, Patrick Hamilton and John Bingham, as well as several Americans among whom the remarkably talented Patricia Highsmith should be particularly mentioned. There has been a loss, certainly, in the collapse of the detective story, and many readers will regret the passing of the Great Detective: but the loss is more than counterbalanced by what has been gained in characterisation, in psychological analysis, and in a more nearly realistic approach to crime and punishment. It may be too soon to announce the death of the detective story: but not, surely, to say *Long live the crime novel*.

THE DETECTIVE STORY IN BRITAIN

A Select Bibliography

(Place of publication London, unless stated otherwise)

NOTE: Many detective story writers have published dozens of books, and a complete list of their works would have occupied a disproportionate amount of space. Consequently, in the case of writers who have published a considerable number of books, or of writers whose work today seems of mainly historical interest, only the most important of their works have been listed, the rest being subsumed under 'And Others'. Otherwise, it is understood that a writer's contributions to detective fiction have been listed in full. One or two items which are not strictly detective stories have been included. The most important of them is Wilkie Collins's *The Woman in White*. This is a thriller; but it would be absurd to exclude what is, by general agreement, one of Collins's most important books.

An asterisk indicates a volume of short stories

Check-List of Authors and Titles:

ALLINGHAM, Margery

The White Cottage Mystery (1928).
The Crime at Black Dudley (1929).
Mystery Mile (1930).
Police at the Funeral (1931).
Look to the Lady (1931).
Sweet Danger (1933).
Death of a Ghost (1934).
Flowers for the Judge (1936).
The Case of the Late Pig (1937).
Dancers in Mourning (1937).
The Fashion in Shrouds (1938).
*Mr. Campion and Others (1939).
Black Plumes (1940).
Traitors' Purse (1941).
Coroner's Pidgin (1945).
More Work for the Undertaker (1948).
The Tiger in the Smoke (1952).
The Beckoning Lady (1955).
Hide my Eyes (1958).

BENNETT, Margot
   Time to Change Hats (1945).
   Away Went the Little Fish (1946).
   The Widow of Bath (1952).
   Farewell Crown and Goodbye King (1953).
   The Man who Didn't Fly (1955).
   Someone from the Past (1958).

BENTLEY, E. C.
   Trent's Last Case (1913)
   —with H. Warner Allen.
   Trent's Own Case (1936).
   *Trent Intervenes (1938).

BERKELEY, Anthony (pseudonym of A. B. Cox).
   The Layton Court Mystery (1925)
   —published anonymously.
   Mr. Priestley's Problem (1927)
   —as by A. B. Cox, later republished under the name of Anthony Berkeley.
   Roger Sheringham and the Vane Mystery (1927).
   The Silk Stocking Murders (1928).
   The Piccadilly Murder (1929).
   The Poisoned Chocolates Case (1929).
   The Second Shot (1930).
   Top Storey Murder (1931).
   Murder in the Basement (1932).
   Jumping Jenny (1933).
   Panic Party (1934).
   Trial and Error (1937).
   Not to be Taken (1938).
   Death in the House (1939).
           See also ILES, Francis below.

BINGHAM, John (Lord Clanmorris).
   My Name is Michael Sibley (1952).
   Five Roundabouts to Heaven (1953).
   The Third Skin (1954).
   The Paton Street Case (1955).
   Marion (1958).
   Murder Plan Six (1958).
   Night's Black Agent (1961).

BLAKE, Nicholas (pseudonym of C. Day Lewis).
  A Question of Proof (1935).
  Thou Shell of Death (1936).
  There's Trouble Brewing (1937).
  The Beast Must Die (1938).
  The Smiler with the Knife (1939).
  Malice in Wonderland (1940).
  The Case of the Abominable Snowman (1941).
  Minute for Murder (1947).
  Head of a Traveller (1949).
  The Dreadful Hollow (1953).
  The Whisper in the Gloom (1954).
  A Tangled Web (1956).
  End of Chapter (1957).
  A Penknife in my Heart (1958).
  The Widow's Cruise (1959).

BRAMAH, Ernest
  *Max Carrados (1914).
  *The Eyes of Max Carrados (1923).
  *Max Carrados Mysteries (1927).

CARR, John Dickson
  It Walks by Night (1930).
  Poison in Jest (1932).
  The Hollow Man (1935).
  The Arabian Nights Murder (1936).
  The Four False Weapons (1937).
  The Burning Court (1937).
  The Crooked Hinge (1938).
  The Black Spectacles (1939).
  The Problem of the Wire Cage (1940).
  The Emperor's Snuff Box (1943).
  He Who Whispers (1946).
  *The Exploits of Sherlock Holmes (1954)
  —with Adrian Conan Doyle.
  And Others
              See also DICKSON, Carter below.

CHESTERTON, G. K.
>   *The Innocence of Father Brown (1911).
>   *The Wisdom of Father Brown (1914).
>   *The Man who Knew too Much (1922).
>   *The Incredulity of Father Brown (1926).
>   *The Secret of Father Brown (1927).
>   *The Poet and the Lunatics (1929).
>   *The Scandal of Father Brown (1935).
>   A selection of Father Brown stories, with an introduction by Ronald Knox, is available in the World's Classics series, 1955.

CHRISTIE, Agatha
>   The Mysterious Affair at Styles (1920).
>   The Secret Adversary (1922).
>   The Murder on the Links (1923).
>   The Man in the Brown Suit (1924).
>   The Secret of Chimneys (1925).
>   The Murder of Roger Ackroyd (1926).
>   Peril at End House (1932).
>   Lord Edgware Dies (1933).
>   Why Didn't They Ask Evans (1934).
>   Murder on the Orient Express (1934).
>   Three Act Tragedy (1935).
>   Murder in Mesopotamia (1936).
>   Cards on the Table (1936).
>   The A.B.C. Murders (1936).
>   Appointment with Death (1938).
>   Ten Little Niggers (1939).
>   N. or M? (1941).
>   Five Little Pigs (1942).
>   The Moving Finger (1943).
>   Towards Zero (1944).
>   Death Comes as the End (1945).
>   Sparkling Cyanide (1945).
>   They do it with Mirrors (1952).
>   After the Funeral (1953).
>   4.50 from Paddington (1957).
>   *And Others*

COLLINS, Wilkie
*After Dark (1856).
The Dead Secret (1857).
The Woman in White (1860).
Hide and Seek (1861).
No Name (1863).
Armadale (1866).
The Moonstone (1868).
And Others

The Moonstone is available in the World's Classics series, with an important introduction by T. S. Eliot; and in Everyman's Library, with an introduction by Dorothy Sayers.

CRISPIN, Edmund (pseudonym of Robert Bruce Montgomery)
The Case of the Gilded Fly (1944).
Holy Disorders (1945).
The Moving Toyshop (1946).
Swan Song (1947).
Love Lies Bleeding (1948).
Buried for Pleasure (1948).
Frequent Hearses (1950).
The Long Divorce (1951).
*Beware of the Trains (1953).

CROFTS, Freeman Wills
The Cask (1920).
The Pit-Prop Syndicate (1922).
The Groote Park Murder (1924).
Inspector French's Greatest Case (1925).
The 12.30 from Croydon (1934).
Death of a Train (1946).
And Others

DICKENS, Charles
Bleak House (1853).
The Mystery of Edwin Drood (1870).
An edition of *Edwin Drood*, with an interesting introduction by Michael Innes, was published in 1950.

DICKSON, Carter (pseudonym of John Dickson Carr).
    The Bowstring Murders (1934).
    The Plague Court Murders (1935).
    The Ten Teacups (1937).
    The Judas Window (1938).
    Death in Five Boxes (1938).
    The Reader is Warned (1939).
    *The Department of Queer Complaints (1940).
    Seeing is Believing (1942).
    He Wouldn't Kill Patience (1944).
    My Late Wives (1947).
    And Others

        See also CARR, John Dickson above.

CONAN DOYLE, Arthur
    A Study in Scarlet (1888)
    —first published in *Beeton's Christmas Annual*, 1887.
    The Sign of Four (1890).
    *The Adventures of Sherlock Holmes (1894).
    The Hound of the Baskervilles (1902).
    *The Return of Sherlock Holmes (1905).
    The Valley of Fear (1915).
    *His Last Bow (1917).
    *The Case-Book of Sherlock Holmes (1927).

FREEMAN, R. Austin
    *John Thorndyke's Cases (1909).
    *The Singing Bone (1912).
    *Dr. Thorndyke's Case-Book (1923).
    The Mystery of Angelina Frood (1924).
    The D'Arblay Mystery (1926).
    Mr. Pottermack's Oversight (1930).

GRIERSON, Edward
    Reputation for a Song (1952).
    The Second Man (1956).

HAMILTON, Patrick
　Hangover Square (1941).

ILES, Francis (pseudonym of A. B. Cox).
　Malice Aforethought (1931).
　Before the Fact (1932).
　As for the Woman (1939).

　　See also BERKELEY, Anthony above.

INNES, Michael (pseudonym of J. I. M. Stewart).
　Death at the President's Lodging (1936).
　Hamlet, Revenge! (1937).
　Lament for a Maker (1938).
　Stop Press (1939).
　There Came Both Mist and Snow (1940).
　Appleby of Ararat (1941).
　The Weight of the Evidence (1944).
　Appleby's End (1945).
　From London Far (1946).
　A Private View (1952).
　The Long Farewell (1958).
　The New Sonia Wayward (1960).
　And Others

KNOX, Ronald
　The Viaduct Murder (1925).
　The Three Taps (1927).
　The Footsteps at the Lock (1928).
　And Others

LE FANU, J. Sheridan
　The House by the Churchyard (1863).
　Wylder's Hand (1864).
　The Wyvern Mystery (1869).
　Checkmate (1871).
　*In a Glass Darkly (1872).

MARSH, Ngaio

>Death in a White Tie (1938).
>Artists in Crime (1938).
>Overture to Death (1939).
>Death at the Bar (1940).
>Death and the Dancing Footman (1942).
>Colour Scheme (1943).
>Died in the Wool (1945).
>Final Curtain (1947).
>Opening Night (1951).
>Scales of Justice (1955).
>Singing in the Shrouds (1959).
>*And Others*

MASON, A. E. W.

>At the Villa Rose (1910).
>The House of the Arrow (1924).
>The Prisoner in the Opal (1928).
>They Wouldn't be Chessmen (1935).

MORRISON, Arthur

>*Martin Hewitt, Investigator (1894).
>*Chronicles of Martin Hewitt (1895).
>*Adventures of Martin Hewitt (1896).
>*The Red Triangle (1903).

ORCZY, Baroness

>*The Old Man in the Corner (1909).
>*Lady Molly of Scotland Yard (1910).
>*Unravelled Knots (1925).
>*Skin o' my Tooth (1928).

POE, Edgar Allan

>Tales (1845).
>Tales of Mystery, Imagination and Horror (1852).
>*Tales of Mystery and Imagination* is published in Everyman's Library, with an introduction by Padraic Colum. Several tales are included also in *The Tell-Tale Heart and Other Stories*, a selection published in 1948, with an introduction by William Sansom.

SAYERS, Dorothy
    Whose Body? (1923).
    Clouds of Witness (1926).
    Unnatural Death (1927).
    Lord Peter Views the Body (1928).
    The Unpleasantness at the Bellona Club (1928).
    Strong Poison (1930).
    The Documents in the Case (1930)
    —with Robert Eustace.
    The Five Red Herrings (1931).
    Have his Carcase (1932).
    *Hangman's Holiday (1933).
    Murder must Advertise (1933).
    The Nine Tailors (1934).
    Gaudy Night (1935).
    Busman's Honeymoon (1937).
    *In the Teeth of the Evidence (1939).

SMITH, Shelley (pseudonym of Nancy Hermione Bodington).
    Come and be Killed (1946).
    He Died of Murder (1947).
    The Woman in the Sea (1948).
    Man Alone (1952).
    An Afternoon to Kill (1953).
    The Lord have Mercy (1956).
    And Others

TEY, Josephine (pseudonym of Elizabeth Mackintosh).
    The Man in the Queue (1929)
    —published under the pseudonym of Gordon Daviot, later republished under the pseudonym Josephine Tey.
    The Franchise Affair (1948).
    Brat Farrar (1949).
    The Daughter of Time (1951).
    The Singing Sands (1952).

Some Critical and Bibliographical Studies:

The following list includes only works bearing upon detective stories in general; it does not cover particular studies (e.g. of Sherlock Holmes and Dr. Watson), or biographies (e.g. of Edgar Allan Poe, Wilkie Collins, Conan Doyle, etc.).

CARTER, John

'Detective Fiction' (1934)
—in *New Paths in Book-Collecting*. Separately issued as *Collecting Detective Fiction*, 1938. This is a short study of primarily bibliographical interest, now inevitably out of date in certain respects, but still of considerable value.

CHESTERTON, G. K.

'A Defence of Detective Stories' (1902)
—in *The Defendant*.
'On Detective Novels' (1928)
—in *Generally Speaking*.
'On Detective Story Writers' (1931)
—in *Come to Think of It*.
These are the best of Chesterton's short essays dealing with detective stories.

GILBERT, Michael (editor)

Crime in Good Company (1959)
—a collection of essays by several members of the Crime Writers' Association.

HAYCRAFT, Howard

Murder for Pleasure (1942)
—with an introduction by Nicholas Blake. This, although it shows perhaps a slight bias towards American writers, is much the best and most comprehensive survey of detective fiction up to the year of its publication.
Notes on Additions to a Cornerstone Library (1951)
—Mr. Haycraft's choice of the best detective stories up to the year 1948. Originally published in *Ellery Queen's Mystery Magazine*, it was later separately issued as *A Decennial Detective Digest*.

KNOX, Ronald
> Introduction to *The Best Detective Stories of 1928* (1929)
> —contains his 'Detective Decalogue'.

MAUGHAM, W. Somerset
> 'The Decline and Fall of the Detective Story' (1952)
> —in *The Vagrant Mood*.

MORLAND, Nigel
> How to write Detective Novels (1936).

MURCH, A. E.
> The Development of the Detective Novel (1958)
> —very good on developments up to around 1914, sketchy in dealing with later work.

QUEEN, Ellery
> Queen's Quorum (1953)
> —a choice of the 101 best books of detective stories, with very interesting notes and commentaries.

SAYERS, Dorothy (editor)
> Introductions to *Great Short Stories of Detection, Mystery and Horror*, First series (1928); Second series (1931); Third series (1934).
> Introduction to *Tales of Detection* (1936)
> —in Everyman's Library.
> Read together, these Introductions form an admirably balanced short history of the detective story up to the dates they were written.

SUTHERLAND, Scott
> Blood in Their Ink (1953)

SYMONS, Julian (editor)
> The 100 Best Crime Stories (1959).
> —a survey first published in the *Sunday Times*.

THOMSON, H. Douglas

   Masters of Mystery (1931)
   —a survey of historical interest, but of very limited value today.

TIMES LITERARY SUPPLEMENT

   Important supplements have been published on 'Detective Fiction' (25 February 1955) and 'Crime, Detection and Society' (23 June 1961).

VAN DINE, S. S.

   The Philo Vance Omnibus (1936)
   —contains his 'Twenty Rules for Writing Detective Stories'.

WRONG, E. M. (editor)

   Introduction to *Crime and Detection* (1926)
   —in the World's Classics series.

WRITERS AND THEIR WORK

General Editor: BONAMY DOBRÉE

The first 55 issues in the Series appeared under the General Editorship of T. O. BEACHCROFT

Sixteenth Century and Earlier:
FRANCIS BACON: J. Max Patrick
CHAUCER: Nevill Coghill
ENGLISH MARITIME WRITING:
    Hakluyt to Cook: Oliver Warner
MALORY: M. C. Bradbrook
MARLOWE: Philip Henderson
SIDNEY: Kenneth Muir
SKELTON: Peter Green
SPENSER: Rosemary Freeman
SIR THOMAS WYATT: Sergio Baldi

Seventeenth Century:
SIR THOMAS BROWNE: Peter Green
BUNYAN: Henri Talon
CAVALIER POETS: Robin Skelton
DONNE: Frank Kermode
DRYDEN: Bonamy Dobrée
HERRICK: John Press
HOBBES: T. E. Jessop
BEN JONSON: J. B. Bamborough
LOCKE: Maurice Cranston
ANDREW MARVELL: John Press
MILTON: E. M. W. Tillyard
SHAKESPEARE: C. J. Sisson
SHAKESPEARE: EARLY COMEDIES:
    Derek Traversi
SHAKESPEARE: GREAT TRAGEDIES:
    Kenneth Muir
SHAKESPEARE: THE PROBLEM
  PLAYS: Peter Ure
THREE METAPHYSICAL POETS:
    Margaret Willy
IZAAK WALTON: Margaret Bottrall

Eighteenth Century:
BERKELEY: T. E. Jessop
BLAKE: Kathleen Raine
BOSWELL: P. A. W. Collins
BURKE: T. E. Utley
BURNS: David Daiches
COWPER: N. Nicholson
CRABBE: R. L. Brett

DEFOE: J. R. Sutherland
ENGLISH HYMNS: Arthur Pollard
FIELDING: John Butt
GIBBON: C. V. Wedgwood
GOLDSMITH: A. Norman Jeffares
GRAY: R. W. Ketton-Cremer
JOHNSON: S. C. Roberts
POPE: Ian Jack
RICHARDSON: R. F. Brissenden
SHERIDAN: W. A. Darlington
SMOLLETT: Laurence Brander
STEELE, ADDISON AND THEIR
  PERIODICAL ESSAYS:
    A. R. Humphreys
STERNE: D. W. Jefferson
SWIFT: J. Middleton Murry
HORACE WALPOLE: Hugh Honour

Nineteenth Century:
MATTHEW ARNOLD: Kenneth Allott
JANE AUSTEN: S. Townsend Warner
THE BRONTË SISTERS:
    Phyllis Bentley
BROWNING: John Bryson
SAMUEL BUTLER: G. D. H. Cole
BYRON: Herbert Read
CARLYLE: David Gascoyne
LEWIS CARROLL: Derek Hudson
COLERIDGE: Kathleen Raine
DICKENS: K. J. Fielding
DISRAELI: Paul Bloomfield
GEORGE ELIOT: Lettice Cooper
ENGLISH TRAVELLERS IN THE NEAR
  EAST: Robin Fedden
FITZGERALD: Joanna Richardson
MRS. GASKELL: Miriam Allott
GISSING: A. C. Ward
THOMAS HARDY: R. A. Scott-James
HAZLITT: J. B. Priestley
G. M. HOPKINS: Geoffrey Grigson
T. H. HUXLEY: William Irvine
KEATS: Edmund Blunden
LAMB: Edmund Blunden

LANDOR: G. Rostrevor Hamilton
MACAULAY: G. R. Potter
JOHN STUART MILL: M. Cranston
WILLIAM MORRIS: P. Henderson
NEWMAN: J. M. Cameron
PATER: Iain Fletcher
ROSSETTI: Oswald Doughty
RUSKIN: Peter Quennell
SIR WALTER SCOTT: Ian Jack
SHELLEY: Stephen Spender
R. L. STEVENSON: G. B. Stern
SWINBURNE: H. J. C. Grierson
TENNYSON: F. L. Lucas
THACKERAY: Laurence Brander
THOMPSON: Peter Butter
TROLLOPE: Hugh Sykes Davies
OSCAR WILDE: James Laver
WORDSWORTH: Helen Darbishire

Twentieth Century:
W. H. AUDEN: Richard Hoggart
HILAIRE BELLOC: Renée Haynes
ARNOLD BENNETT: F. Swinnerton
EDMUND BLUNDEN: Alec M. Hardie
ELIZABETH BOWEN: Jocelyn Brooke
ROY CAMPBELL: David Wright
JOYCE CARY: Walter Allen
G. K. CHESTERTON: C. Hollis
WINSTON CHURCHILL: John Connell
R. G. COLLINGWOOD:
            E. W. F. Tomlin
L. COMPTON-BURNETT:
            Pamela Hansford Johnson
JOSEPH CONRAD: Oliver Warner
WALTER DE LA MARE: K. Hopkins
NORMAN DOUGLAS: Ian Greenlees
T. S. ELIOT: M. C. Bradbrook
ENGLISH TRANSLATORS AND
    TRANSLATIONS: J. M. Cohen
FORD MADOX FORD: Kenneth Young

E. M. FORSTER: Rex Warner
CHRISTOPHER FRY: Derek Stanfo
JOHN GALSWORTHY: R. H. Mott
ROBERT GRAVES: M. Seymour S
GRAHAM GREENE: Francis Wynd
A. E. HOUSMAN: Ian Scott-Kilve
ALDOUS HUXLEY: Jocelyn Brook
HENRY JAMES: Michael Swan
JAMES JOYCE: J. I. M. Stewart
RUDYARD KIPLING: B. Dobrée
D. H. LAWRENCE: Kenneth You
C. DAY LEWIS: Clifford Dyment
WYNDHAM LEWIS: E. W. F. To
KATHERINE MANSFIELD: Ian Go
JOHN MASEFIELD: L. A. G. Stro
SOMERSET MAUGHAM: J. Broph
EDWIN MUIR: J. C. Hall
J. MIDDLETON MURRY: Philip M
GEORGE ORWELL: Tom Hopkins
POETS OF THE 1939-45 WAR:
            R. N. Cu
J. B. PRIESTLEY: Ivor Brown
HERBERT READ: Francis Berry
BERTRAND RUSSELL: Alan Dor
BERNARD SHAW: A. C. Ward
EDITH SITWELL: John Lehmann
OSBERT SITWELL: Roger Fulfor
C. P. SNOW: William Cooper
LYTTON STRACHEY:
            R. A. Scott-J
DYLAN THOMAS: G. S. Fraser
G. M. TREVELYAN: J. H. Plumb
WAR POETS: 1914-18:
            Edmund Blu
EVELYN WAUGH: Christopher H
H. G. WELLS: Montgomery Belg
CHARLES WILLIAMS:
            John Heath-St
VIRGINIA WOOLF: Bernard Black
W. B. YEATS: G. S. Fraser

In Preparation:

SHAKESPEARE: THE CHRONICLES:
            Clifford Leech
ARTHUR HUGH CLOUGH:
            Isobel Armstrong

J. M. SYNGE and LADY GREGOR
            Elizabeth Co
ROBERT BRIDGES: John Sparro